Mr Bean

RICHARD CURTIS and ROBIN DRISCOLL

Level 2

Retold by Joanna Strange
Series Editors: Andy Hopkins and Jocelyn Potter

W9-BGK-131

Pearson Education Limited
Edinburgh Gate, Harlow,
Essex CM20 2JE, England
and Associated Companies throughout the world.

ISBN 0 582 34129 9

First published by Boxtree 1997
This edition first published 2000

Text copyright © Robin Driscoll, Richard Curtis, Rowan Atkinson 1997, 2000
Photographs copyright © Polygram Filmed Entertainment Limited 1997, 2000

Typeset by Digital Type, London
Set in 11/14pt Bembo
Printed in Spain by Mateu Cromo, S. A. Pinto (Madrid)

Published by Pearson Education Limited in association with
Penguin Books Ltd, both companies being subsidiaries of Pearson Plc

Acknowledgements:
All photographs by Liam Daniel, Suzanne Hanover and Melissa Moseley

For a complete list of the titles available in the Penguin Readers series please write to your local
Pearson Education office or to: Marketing Department, Penguin Longman Publishing,
5 Bentinck Street, London W1M 5RN.

Contents

Introduction

Mr Bean! Nobody in the room liked Mr Bean – they all wanted him to leave the gallery. Why? What was wrong with the man? He only had to sit in one of the rooms in the gallery all day and watch the paintings. He wasn't very good at his job – he usually fell asleep. But why did they all hate him?

In Los Angeles, a famous painting by an American artist is coming to the Grierson Gallery. Everybody at the gallery is very excited. They want a top man from England to come to America. He can talk about the artist and his painting when they show it to people. Who is the National Gallery in London going to send for this important job? Mr Bean, of course!

But something is very wrong with Mr Bean! What is it? He's *very, very* strange. And dangerous! Accidents start to happen when he gets on the plane to Los Angeles. After he arrives, things get worse and worse and worse . . .

Richard Curtis and Robin Driscoll wrote the film, *Bean*, in 1995. Rowan Atkinson plays Mr Bean and it is a very funny film. When it came out in 1997, a lot of people saw it at cinemas round the world.

You can see Rowan Atkinson as Mr Bean on television and video, but Richard Curtis always wanted to write a Mr Bean film for the cinema. He thought about the idea for two years before he started writing it. His other films, *Four Weddings and a Funeral* and *Notting Hill*, are very famous too.

Chapter 1   A Great Day!

Everybody at the Grierson Art Gallery in Los Angeles was very excited.

George Grierson, the boss, stood outside the gallery and looked at the people in front of him. He smiled and turned to the cameras.

'This is a great day for the Grierson Gallery, and a great day for America,' he said. 'In two weeks, the most famous painting by an American artist is coming back home. Yes, everybody, America's most wonderful painting, *Whistler's Mother*, will be here in *my* gallery!'

♦

At the National Gallery in London, everybody was very excited too.

The Grierson Gallery wanted somebody from London to go to America for two months. They wanted a top man from the National Gallery to talk to people about the artist, Whistler,★ and his famous painting of his mother.

Who was the right person for the job? Dr Rosenblum? Or Dr Cutler? At a meeting in one of the rooms in the gallery, everybody wanted to go.

But first they had to discuss a more important problem: Mr Bean! Nobody in the room liked Mr Bean – they all wanted him to leave the gallery. Why? What was wrong with the man? He only had to sit in one of the rooms in the gallery all day and

★ James McNeill Whistler (1834–1903): A famous artist. He was American, but he lived in London.

He wasn't very good at his job — he usually fell asleep.

watch the paintings. He wasn't very good at his job – he usually fell asleep. But why did they *all* hate him?

Suddenly, the National Gallery's boss, Mr Walton, came into the room and sat down at the table.

'We're talking about that strange man, Mr Bean, sir,' somebody said. 'We all think . . .'

'Be quiet!' shouted Mr Walton angrily. 'There's nothing wrong with Mr Bean! He's a wonderful young man – one of the best men in the gallery.'

Nobody in the room said a word. They all looked very unhappy.

'Wait a minute!' somebody suddenly shouted. 'Of course! Why don't we send Mr Bean to the Grierson Gallery in America?'

Nobody spoke. It was a stupid idea! Or was it? Mr Bean in America! Two long months without the man!

'Yes, yes!' they all shouted. 'That's a great idea!'

Mr Walton looked very happy. 'Right. Don't sit there! Get Mr Bean! Quickly!'

♦

Mr Bean sat and waited outside the room. Why did these important people want to see him? Suddenly, he sneezed loudly. He took out a paper handkerchief and blew his nose. Then he blew it again. Then again, more loudly – the noisiest nose-blow in the world!

Mr Walton called Mr Bean into the room. When he walked in, he smiled at everybody. They all looked at him . . . and started laughing! Mr Bean looked *very* stupid!

'Excuse me, Mr Bean,' Mr Walton said, 'um . . . ah . . . something's coming out of your nose!'

It was some of his paper handkerchief! It looked very funny! Mr Bean's face went red and he quickly pulled the paper out of his nose.

They all looked at him . . . and started laughing!

'Now, Mr Bean. We want to ask you something. It's important – and very exciting. Would you like to go to America?'

Chapter 2   An Accident on the Plane

'Americaaaaaa!!' shouted Mr Bean at the airport. 'I'm going to Americaaaaaa!!'

With a big smile on his face, he got on the plane and took out his camera. This was the beginning of his holiday and he wanted to take photos of everybody and everything.

He found his seat next to another man, Mr Tucker. Mr Bean sat down and took a photo of him too! Mr Tucker stopped reading his newspaper and looked at him angrily. Then he stood up and quickly moved to the seat in front of him. He didn't like strange people – and Mr Bean was *very* strange! Happy in his new seat, Mr Tucker fell asleep.

Behind him, Mr Bean couldn't sleep. He was too excited. He smiled at a woman with a young boy, but she didn't smile at him.

'My son's feeling sick,' she said.

'Oh dear!' said Mr Bean. He was happy, and he wanted other people to be happy too.

When the boy looked across at him, Mr Bean took the last sweet from a bag. He threw it into the air – and caught it in his mouth!

Did the boy think it was clever? No. Did the boy laugh or smile? He did not. He looked strangely at Mr Bean.

Mr Bean thought for a minute. Then he put the sweet bag up to his mouth and began to blow into it. He wanted to blow air into the bag and then break it with a loud noise – BANG! Everybody laughs at that. But there was something wrong with the bag and the air got out again.

The boy's face was grey now, and he felt very sick. Then he saw a white paper bag in the back of the seat in front of him. He took it out and opened it.

Mr Bean watched him. His eyes opened wide. Yes! Yes! *That* bag was OK! He turned away and laughed. 'He's a clever boy. He remembered the bag in the back of the seat!' he thought.

But Mr Bean looked away at the wrong time. The boy opened the bag quickly – and was sick into it. Mr Bean didn't see him.

A minute later, before the boy could stop him, Mr Bean took the bag. He quickly blew into it. Then he put it in front of Mr Tucker's face. With the bag in one hand and a big smile on his face, Mr Bean hit it hard – BANG!

Mr Tucker was not a happy man.

♦

Some time later, the plane arrived in Los Angeles. Mr Bean looked at the people in the airport.

'I'm in America!' he thought. 'This is wonderful!'

He started taking photos again. Near a wall there were two policemen. Mr Bean watched them, and then he saw their guns. He thought of a game, and smiled. He put one hand slowly inside his jacket and looked for *his* gun. Not really! Mr Bean didn't have a gun, of course – he only wanted to play a game.

The two policemen suddenly turned and saw him. They stopped talking and looked carefully at Mr Bean. What was this little man's game? Did he have a gun?

'Quick!' said one of the policemen. 'He's got a gun! Get him!'

Mr Bean gave them a smile. Then he turned and ran the other way, fast!

'Everybody on the floor! Now!' shouted the policemen.

Everybody in the airport was afraid. People fell to the ground. Mr Bean saw them and fell to the ground too!

'Not you, stupid!' a man next to him said.

'Oh, thank you,' said Mr Bean. He got up and started to run away again.

But the policemen ran faster and caught him. They stood in front of him with their guns in his face.

The policemen stood with their guns in his face.

He carefully put his hand in his jacket . . . and took out his two fingers.

'Slowly take out your gun,' they told him. 'Put it on the floor and stand back.'

Mr Bean was very afraid. He carefully put his hand in his jacket . . . and took out his two fingers.

'It was only a game,' he said. 'I haven't really got a gun.'

The policemen looked at him. Who *was* this strange little man?

'Get out of here!' they shouted angrily.

Mr Bean got out, fast.

Chapter 3   Wet Trousers!

The Langleys were usually a very happy family. They lived in a large house in Los Angeles. David Langley had an important job at the Grierson Gallery. His wife, Alison, was a friendly, intelligent woman. They had two lovely children – a fifteen-year-old daughter, Jennifer, and a seven-year-old son, Kevin.

One day, David came home from the gallery and said to his family, 'Listen! I've got a great idea! A top man from the National Gallery in London is coming to Los Angeles. I'd like to invite him here. He can stay with us for two months.'

David's family didn't like the idea very much. Who was this man? A boring Englishman? No thank you!

'Here? In our house? For two months?' Alison said. 'No, David! He can stay in a hotel.'

'*I'd* like it,' David answered angrily. 'He's a very intelligent man. It'll be good for all of us.'

So Alison Langley and the children waited for the Englishman's visit.

♦

The big day arrived. Mr Bean was late – problems with the police at the airport – but now he was here in the Langleys' sitting-room.

They all looked at him and smiled. He didn't *look* very intelligent. He looked very strange! Was there something wrong with him? Perhaps he was tired after the long journey from England.

♦

The next morning, David took Mr Bean to the Grierson Gallery.

'My boss, Mr Grierson, would like to meet you at nine o'clock,' he told Mr Bean in the car. 'And he gets angry when people are late, Dr Bean.'

Mr Bean sat in the car and looked out of the window. Why did David call him *Doctor* Bean, not *Mr* Bean? Doctor was the name for the top men in the National Gallery – Dr Rosenblum and Dr Cutler. They were very intelligent and knew a lot about art. He didn't know anything about art. But he felt very important when David called him Dr Bean!

When they got to the gallery, Mr Bean wanted to go to the toilet. David looked at his watch.

'The Men's Room is over there, Dr Bean. But please, don't be too long. Mr Grierson's waiting . . .'

Mr Bean walked into the Men's Room. He went to the toilet and then started to wash his hands. But the water went everywhere – over the front of his trousers!

'Oh no!' he thought. 'What am I going to do? I can't meet Mr Grierson with wet trousers!'

Then he saw a machine on the wall.

'Aah, good, a hand-dryer,' he thought. 'That'll dry them in no time.'

Mr Bean jumped up and down, but the machine was too high. The warm air didn't blow on to his trousers.

Then he had an idea. He climbed on to a chair in front of the machine and started to move slowly from left to right. The warm air blew on to his trousers in the right place.

Suddenly, a man came out of one of the toilets. He looked up and saw Mr Bean. Then he walked out as fast as possible!

David Langley stood outside the Men's Room and waited for Mr Bean. He looked at his watch. It was after nine o'clock.

'Dr Bean, we're late,' he shouted. 'Mr Grierson will be very angry.'

Mr Bean came out of the Men's Room and followed David. This wasn't funny! His trousers weren't dry – he wanted more time in front of the hand-dryer. He couldn't go into Mr Grierson's office with wet trousers! Then he saw a newspaper on a table. He took the paper and put it in front of his trousers.

Mr Grierson's office was a beautiful room. There were paintings everywhere – and on the wall behind the desk was a

He climbed on to a chair in front of the machine and started to move slowly from left to right.

big poster of *Whistler's Mother*. There were a lot of important people in the room.

Mr Grierson looked at his watch. 'Ah, David, good morning. And this is our famous Dr Bean from England! How are you, Dr Bean?'

Mr Bean said hello to everybody in the room.

'Now, sit down, Dr Bean,' said Mr Grierson, and took the newspaper out of his hands.

Mr Bean sat down quickly. He didn't want these important people to see his wet trousers!

Everybody sat round the table and the meeting began. But Mr Bean didn't listen to a word. He couldn't stop thinking about his trousers. What *could* he do?

He saw a fan. Ah! He got up, and moved slowly across the room. Then he started dancing in front of the fan!

Then he started dancing in front of the fan!

Everybody in the room stopped talking and looked at him. 'What *is* the man doing?' they thought.

Mr Bean looked down at his trousers. Good! They were dry! He turned round and smiled at everybody. Then he walked slowly back to his seat – he wanted them to see the front of his lovely dry trousers!

'Yes . . . right . . . um . . . Dr Bean,' said Mr Grierson. 'Please, sit down . . . Now, when *Whistler's Mother* arrives at the gallery, we want you to say something. About twenty minutes will be fine. You know, talk about the artist and his work. OK?'

Mr Bean didn't understand! Him? Say something? But he didn't know anything about art!

'Er . . . yes . . . of course,' he said.

♦

The meeting ended and everybody stood up. Mr Grierson talked quietly to David.

'This Dr Bean, David – he's the National Gallery's top man, right?'

'That's right, sir,' David answered.

'Good. This painting, *Whistler's Mother*, is very important to the gallery. You know that. I don't want anything to go wrong. Do you understand me, David?'

'I understand, sir,' said David.

He smiled at his boss, but he didn't feel very happy.

Chapter 4   At the Fairground

That evening, David came home and walked into the kitchen.

'Hi, Ali,' he said, and put his arm round his wife.

'Hi,' answered Alison.

She looked behind David carefully and then smiled.

'Oh good! No Dr Bean! I didn't like having that man in our house, dear.'

'Ah ... he isn't here now ... but I'm sorry, dear ... he's coming,' said David.

'What? Jennifer! Kevin!' Alison shouted. 'It's Plan B!'

'What's Plan B, Ali?' asked David.

'Plan B is this, David,' Alison said. 'The children and I are not going to stay in the same house as Dr Bean. He's too strange! He makes funny faces! He throws sweets up in the air and catches them in his mouth! He broke my best picture! He's a very dangerous little man! We're going to my mother's for the weekend!'

'But, Ali, wait a minute ...' David cried.

But he was too late. Alison and the two children were in her car. He watched them drive away.

'Oh no!' he thought. 'Dr Bean will be here all weekend, and I'll have no help from anybody!'

♦

The next day was Saturday and Mr Bean wanted to see Los Angeles. When he got into David's car, he took out his camera.

'Great!' he shouted excitedly. 'I'm going to enjoy today!'

David drove through the city and Mr Bean took photos of everything and everybody – people, buildings, policemen, dogs, trees, flowers. He was very busy! Then he put the camera up in front of David's face and took some photos of him too.

'Stop that!' shouted David. 'It's dangerous! I'm trying to drive!'

In the afternoon, they stopped at a fairground in Santa Monica, near Los Angeles. There were rides and sweet shops and people in funny hats. Mr Bean bought an ice-cream and a hat.

There were rides and sweet shops and people in funny hats.

'Oh, this is wonderful!' he shouted, and he took more and more photos. 'Look, David, that ride says "REALLY DANGEROUS". Let's go on that.'

The ride was very exciting. It went up and down very fast. Everybody cried and shouted. David was afraid.

'That wasn't really dangerous. It was really *boring*,' Mr Bean said at the end.

They left the ride and walked past the machine room. Mr Bean saw the computers and machines in the room – and had an idea!

'David, let's go on that ride again,' he said. 'Go and buy some more tickets.'

'OK,' said David unhappily. He felt sick and wanted to go home.

Mr Bean walked into the machine room. Good, nobody there! He sat down and started to work on the computers!

'The ride *will* be "REALLY DANGEROUS" now!' he laughed.

Some minutes later, David and Mr Bean were in their seats again, ready for the same ride. And this time everybody was *really* afraid! People flew out of their seats into the air – but Mr Bean enjoyed every minute of it!

When they got off the ride, he looked at David. David's face was green.

'That was great!' laughed Mr Bean. 'Those computers are much better now!'

But he didn't see the policeman behind him.

♦

Later that afternoon, in the police station, Mr Bean stopped laughing.

'What did you do to those computers, you stupid little man?' the policeman shouted. 'You hurt a lot of people!'

15

Then he made funny faces!

Mr Bean looked down at the floor and said nothing. The policeman walked angrily out of the room.

Mr Bean looked up and saw a mirror. He stood up and started dancing in front of it. Then he made funny faces! But it was a two-way mirror. In the next room, the policeman and David stood behind the mirror and watched Mr Bean.

'You say he's a top man from the National Gallery in London?' asked the policeman.

'Er . . . yes,' said David.

'And he's very intelligent?'

'Yes . . . um . . .'

'He doesn't look very intelligent to me,' said the policeman. 'He looks *very, very* stupid! Now, get him out of here! Fast!'

Chapter 5   A Bad Day at the Gallery

It was a long, difficult weekend for David. Then Monday arrived. The big day at the Grierson Gallery!

In the car on the way to the gallery, David said to Mr Bean, '*Whistler's Mother* is arriving today! There are going to be a lot of important people at the gallery.'

When Mr Bean didn't answer, David looked at him.

Oh no! Mr Bean had a cigarette lighter up his nose!

'*Please*, Dr Bean, *please*! Don't do anything dangerous today! *Please*!' David said. He really didn't want to lose his job!

♦

David and Mr Bean walked into a big room in the gallery. There, at the end of the room, was *Whistler's Mother*!

Oh no! Mr Bean had a cigarette lighter up his nose!

'Wonderful!' said David, when he saw the painting.

Mr Grierson was there and smiled at him.

'Yes, it's very beautiful,' he said. 'A really great work of art. Now, follow me, everybody. We've got to plan the day.'

He turned to Mr Bean. 'Ah, good morning, Dr Bean. Would you like to stay here and look after the painting?'

'Er . . . yes . . . OK,' said Mr Bean.

Then everybody left – and Mr Bean was the only person in the room with the famous painting!

He was bored. He didn't want to look after Whistler's stupid old mother. He started to walk slowly round the room. When he got near the painting, he looked at it carefully.

'This painting's dirty!' he thought, with his face very near the painting.

And then he sneezed! All over the painting! Oh dear!

And then he sneezed! All over the painting!

He quickly got his handkerchief out of his jacket – and started to clean the painting.

'Aagh!' he shouted a minute later. 'Oh no! How did that happen?'

There was now blue ink all over Mrs Whistler's face!

He looked at his handkerchief. There was wet ink on that too!

'My pen!' he cried, and took out his pen from his jacket.

There was ink everywhere. What could he do?

He thought for a minute, then took the painting off the wall. But it was very heavy and fell on to the floor. Then, by mistake, Mr Bean stood on it!

'Help!' he thought. 'This is getting worse and worse!'

He opened the door and looked out of the room. There was nobody there. With great difficulty, he carried the painting out of the room.

'The toilet!' he thought. 'Water!'

He got the painting into the Men's Room, and started to wash it. There was no blue ink now – but where was Mrs Whistler's face?

Mr Bean went hot and cold. Then he had an idea!

♦

The meeting finished, and David left the room.

'Right,' he thought. 'Now I'll get Dr Bean and have another look at our beautiful painting.'

But when he arrived at the room, he couldn't open the door.

'Dr Bean,' he shouted. 'There's a problem with the door. Can you open it, please?'

After a long time, Mr Bean opened the door. David looked at him. Mr Bean's face was grey.

'What's wrong?' he asked.

'Er . . . um . . .,' answered Mr Bean.

'What? What?' cried David.

19

'I painted a face on her. Do you like it?'

Mr Bean looked very afraid.

'It's . . . um . . . it's the painting,' he said quietly.

'Where is it?' shouted David.

'Um . . . here,' said Mr Bean. He showed David the painting. 'I had a little accident. But I think it's OK now. I painted a face on her. Do you like it?'

David looked at the painting with wide eyes. He felt sick.

'Oh no!' he cried. 'No! No! No! What are we going to do *now*?'

Chapter 6   A Good Night's Work

It was midnight in the Langleys' house. Alison and the children were home again. They didn't want to be in the same house as the strange Dr Bean, but the children had to go to school. David was asleep in the sitting-room. Alison was very angry with him and didn't want him in the bedroom.

Mr Bean couldn't sleep. He was very unhappy. He sat in the kitchen. He thought and thought.

'David will lose his job now!' he thought sadly.

At one o'clock, Kevin walked into the kitchen. He looked sleepy.

'Hi, Beanie.'

'Oh, hello, Kevin. Why aren't you in bed?'

'I couldn't sleep. I can't stop thinking about beautiful women with no clothes on! And you?' said Kevin.

'I can't stop thinking about *Whistler's Mother*,' answered Mr Bean.

'*Whistler's Mother*!? Boring! Come up to my room, Beanie,' said Kevin. 'I've got a great poster of Cindy Crawford up there. She's better than old *Whistler's Mother*!'

Then he got a glass of milk and some chocolate cake. 'See you in the morning, Beanie!'

Kevin went back to bed, but Mr Bean sat at the kitchen table. He started thinking again.

A poster of Cindy Crawford? Really! Young people today!

'Wait a minute!' he thought.

Mr Bean suddenly had an idea – another wonderful Mr Bean idea!

He stood up quickly and found a large bag in a cupboard. First, he ran out of the kitchen and into the bathroom with the bag in his hands. Then he went quietly into Alison's bedroom, then into the kitchen again, and then into the garage. After ten minutes, the bag was very heavy – there was a hairdryer in it, a bicycle light, some eggs, some small bottles, and a lot of other things.

Next, Mr Bean went into the sitting-room.

'Now, where's David's card?' he thought. 'I can't open the front door at the gallery without it.'

He found the card in David's jacket and put it in the bag with the other things.

Then Mr Bean put on a black shirt, black jeans and a black hat. He put the bag on his back, and jumped on to Kevin's bicycle. Then he rode quickly out of the garage, into the dark.

♦

Fifteen minutes later, Mr Bean arrived at the Grierson Gallery. He opened the front door with David's card and walked quietly into the building. It was two o'clock in the morning. Nobody saw him.

'Now – where's the gallery shop?' he thought.

He found the shop on the second floor. He carefully opened the door and went in.

'Great!' he thought, when he saw a big poster of *Whistler's Mother*. He put the poster in his bag.

He then found the room with the famous painting – the painting of *Whistler's Mother* with the funny face! He put his bag down on the floor.

'Right, let's start work,' he thought.

It was dark in the room. Mr Bean took Kevin's bicycle light out of the bag and turned it on. Then he took out the poster of *Whistler's Mother*. He looked at the poster and then at the famous painting on the wall.

'I've got to put a new surface on the poster,' he thought. 'Then it'll be the same as the painting.'

He sat on the floor and slowly started painting a new surface on to the poster. He used the eggs from the Langleys' kitchen and things from Alison's bottles.

It was a long, difficult job. After two hours, Mr Bean stood up and looked at the poster.

'Now – where's the gallery shop?' he thought.

'Mmm . . . that's better!' he said with a smile on his face.

He took out the hairdryer from the bag, and dried the new surface. Then he carefully took the famous painting off the wall. He put the poster with the new surface on the wall in the same place.

'Nobody will know it's only a poster!' he thought.

Then Mr Bean put everything back in his bag. He carried the bag and the old painting with the funny face out of the room.

Out in the street, Mr Bean jumped on to Kevin's bicycle and rode back to the Langleys' house. It was five o'clock in the morning.

'A good night's work,' he thought when he got into bed. 'David will be happy now!'

Chapter 7   Clever Dr Bean!

The next morning, at breakfast time, David came slowly into the kitchen. His face looked old and tired.

'It's going to be a bad day today,' he said. 'A *very* bad day!'

In the car, on the way to the gallery, Mr Bean tried to talk to David. He wanted to tell him about the painting.

'Um . . . David . . .'

'Don't talk to me! I *hate* you!' answered David angrily.

'But David . . .' said Mr Bean.

'Quiet!' shouted David. 'Don't say anything! Or I'll kill you! OK?'

Outside the gallery, there were a lot of cars, people and cameras. Everybody wanted to see Whistler's famous painting of his mother. Inside, in the room with the painting, there were about a hundred important people from television and the newspapers.

Nobody could see the painting – they could only see the back of it.

Then he carefully took the famous painting off the wall.

David and Mr Bean walked into the room. David wanted to find Mr Grierson as quickly as possible. He had to tell him about the accident with the painting!

'Ah, David,' said Mr Grierson. 'And Dr Bean. Late again!'

'Sorry, sir. A problem at home. Please sir, I've got to talk to you. Now! It's very important!'

'Not now, David,' Mr Grierson answered. 'Everybody's waiting. We've got to show them the painting!'

'But sir,' cried David, 'it's about the painting.'

But Mr Grierson didn't listen.

Mr Bean looked at David. 'Um . . . David . . .'

'Bean, go away!' David said.

Mr Grierson walked to the front of the room.

'Good morning, everybody,' he said. 'This is a great day for America – and for *Whistler's Mother*. I won't say too much because I know you all want to see our famous painting. And here it is!'

David shut his eyes. 'I'm going to be sick,' he thought.

There wasn't a sound in the room. All eyes were on the back of the painting behind Mr Grierson. He slowly turned the painting round . . .

David stood at the back of the room, next to Mr Bean. He didn't understand! The painting looked wonderful! No blue ink! No funny face! There was nothing wrong with it!

'What? What did you do, Bean?' he said quietly. 'You're wonderful! I love you!'

'Easy!' said Mr Bean. 'It's a poster!'

'It's a what!!!?? But . . . but . . . but . . .'

'Ssh! Somebody will hear!'

'But . . . how did you do it?'

'I came here in the middle of the night and took a poster from the shop,' said Mr Bean. 'I painted a new surface on it with eggs and things. Then I dried it with a hairdryer! What's the problem?'

David stood at the back of the room, next to Mr Bean.

'But . . . you can't . . .'

'Ssh! Don't tell anybody!' laughed Mr Bean. 'Nobody will know it's only a poster!'

'Dr Bean, are you ready?' asked Mr Grierson.

Mr Bean didn't understand.

'Ready for what?' he asked.

'You're going to say something to these people. Don't you remember?'

'What shall I talk about?'

'About the painting, of course,' laughed Mr Grierson. This man was *very* strange!

'Ah! Yes, of course,' said Mr Bean.

He went to the front of the room and smiled at the people and cameras. What did they want him to say?

'We're ready,' said Mr Grierson. 'You can start now.'

'Ahm ... um ... um .... Ahm ... thank you ... and hello, everybody. I'm Mr ... sorry, *Dr* Bean and I work at the National Gallery in London. I sit and look at paintings all day.'

Everybody liked that. They all smiled.

'He's very intelligent,' they thought.

'Now, what can I say about this painting?' said Mr Bean, and he looked at the famous *Whistler's Mother*. 'First ... it's ... um ... very big. I like big paintings.'

Very clever! This man from London was *really* good!

'Next ... and I'm nearly at the end now ... next is the big question. Why did this gallery pay thousands of dollars for this painting?'

Mr Bean looked at David. But David couldn't help him now.

'And ... the answer is ... ahm ... what *is* the answer? This painting is expensive because ... it's a picture of Whistler's mother. And I know ... that families are very important. I know that because I'm staying with my best friend, David, and his lovely family. Whistler's mother wasn't a beautiful woman. Look at the painting – she's an ugly old thing! But she was his mother and he loved her. And I think that's wonderful!'

Everybody stood up.

'Thank you, Dr Bean!'

'Another photo, please!'

'Look this way, Dr Bean!'

Mr Bean was famous! And David was very, very happy.

But before David and Mr Bean could leave the room, a policeman came in.

'Mr Langley?' he asked David. 'Can I talk to you, sir?'

David looked at Mr Bean. He was suddenly very afraid.

'It's OK,' he said to the policeman quickly. 'I'll tell you everything ...'

'Everything?'

'Yes, everything about the painting.'

'What painting? I don't want to talk about a painting,' said the policeman. 'I'm sorry, Mr Langley. It's your daughter. She's in hospital. A road accident, sir.'

Chapter 8   At the Hospital

The hospital was very busy. David and Mr Bean ran quickly to the front desk.

'Excuse me,' David said, 'can you tell me my daughter's room number? Jennifer Langley. She came in at about one o'clock. A road accident.'

'One minute, sir,' said the woman at the desk. 'Ah, yes. She's in Room 106.'

David ran up the stairs. Mr Bean followed him.

'No, Bean!' shouted David. 'You stay there! And *do* nothing! *Nothing* – then nothing can go wrong!'

Mr Bean understood. He watched David leave. He felt very sad. He wanted to help, and he wanted a family too!

David found Room 106 and went in. Jennifer was in bed and Alison was on a chair next to her.

'Ali, how is she?'

'Oh David! I don't know!' cried Alison. 'I'm waiting for the doctor.'

◆

Mr Bean sat and waited for David. After some time, he felt bored and started to walk round the hospital. A doctor suddenly ran out of a room and saw Mr Bean.

'Who are you?' he asked.

'Me? I'm Dr Bean.'

'Good! I'm Dr Jacobson. I want some help, doctor. Come with me.'

Oh no! Mr Bean wasn't really a doctor! He was only Dr Bean at the Grierson Gallery! Not in a hospital!

'Ahm . . . um . . . I'm really *Mr* Bean, not Dr . . .' he said, but Dr Jacobson was too busy. He didn't hear him.

Mr Bean followed Dr Jacobson into an operating room.

'OK, listen everybody. This is Dr Bean. Doctor, this man's got a bullet in his stomach. It's bad! I've got another operation in Room 4 but I'll see you later.'

Dr Jacobson ran out of the operating room – and everybody looked at 'Doctor' Bean!

'Here, doctor, put these clothes on,' somebody said.

'Doctor, this man's dying! Do something! Fast!' another person said.

Mr Bean didn't answer.

'Shall I make the first cut, Dr Bean?' asked a very young doctor.

'OK,' said Mr Bean. He felt very, very afraid.

The young doctor started to cut open the man's stomach. Mr Bean watched and felt very sick.

Suddenly somebody outside shouted, 'Quick! Help! We're losing her! Help!'

Everybody in the operating room ran out . . . and Mr Bean was the only person in the room, again!

He waited for the other people, but nobody came back.

After some time, he took out a packet of sweets. He threw a sweet up into the air and tried to catch it in his mouth. But the sweet fell into the stomach of the man on the operating table!

Mr Bean looked down. He really wanted that sweet! Slowly, he put his hand into the man's stomach. He found the sweet – and took it out.

But it wasn't his sweet! It was the bullet!

Mr Bean was hungry but he couldn't eat a bullet! He quickly put it back into the man's stomach – and then found his sweet. He washed it – and put it into his mouth! Mmmm! Lovely!

A minute later, everybody ran back into the operating room.

'OK! Let's find that bullet!' said the young doctor.

He looked in the man's stomach but he couldn't see it.

'I can't see anything! Where *is* that bullet? We'll have to find it or he's a dead man!'

Mr Bean watched him. He thought for a minute and then said, 'No problem. Here, I'll do it.'

He carefully put his hands into the man's stomach.

Everybody shouted, 'Stop! You can't do that! Take your hands out! It's too dangerous!'

Mr Bean didn't listen. He took his hands out of the man's stomach and smiled. He showed them the bullet!

'What? I don't understand!' cried the young doctor.

'Wonderful! Wonderful!' they all shouted. 'Doctor Bean's the cleverest doctor in the world!'

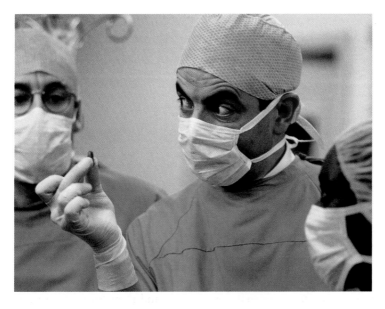

He showed them the bullet!

Chapter 9   'We love you, Mr Bean!'

Five minutes later, Mr Bean walked out of the operating room in
his blue doctor's clothes.

'Phew! I'd like a cup of coffee!' he thought.

Suddenly somebody behind him shouted, 'Doctor! Doctor!'

'Oh, no!' thought Mr Bean. 'Not again!'

He turned round – and there was David!

'Doctor! Come quickly! It's my daughter! She's in Room 106.
Quick!'

Mr Bean couldn't say no. He had to go and see Jennifer.

'Oh, doctor!' cried Alison when she saw Mr Bean in his
doctor's clothes. 'Quick! Do something!'

Mr Bean looked at Jennifer on the bed.

'Aah . . . Mr and Mrs . . .,' he started to say.

'Langley,' said David and Alison.

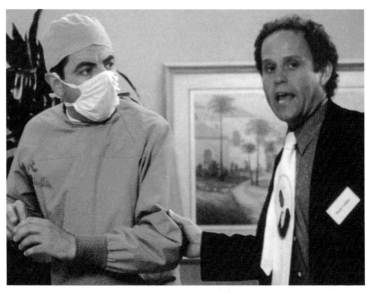

He turned round – and there was David!

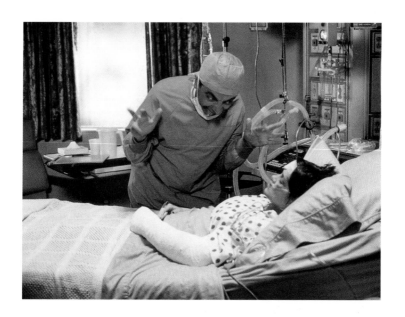

Then he started making funny faces!

'Yes . . . Mr and Mrs Langley . . . um . . . Your daughter's going to be fine but . . . um . . . I'd like to see her without you here.'

'Of course, doctor,' they said, and left quickly.

Mr Bean was the only person in the room – again!

Everything was very quiet. Not a sound. Mr Bean slowly went to Jennifer's bed.

'Jennifer,' he said, 'wake up . . . wake up . . . wake up . . .'

Jennifer didn't open her eyes. Mr Bean sat on the bed and put his face near Jennifer's. Then he started making funny faces!

'Bah!' he shouted. 'Aaagh!'

Jennifer didn't move.

Next Mr Bean hit her. Nothing happened.

He climbed on to her bed and looked down at her. Then he jumped on top of her – hard.

And Jennifer woke up!

'Dad! Mum! Help!' she shouted.

Mr Bean got off the bed quickly.

Outside, David and Alison heard their daughter. They ran into the room as fast as they could.

'Jennifer!' cried Alison. 'You're OK!'

'What happened, mum?' Jennifer asked. Her eyes were wide open now.

'You had an accident, dear. But everything's going to be OK now.'

Mr Bean watched the happy family, then walked to the door. David looked round.

'Doctor, don't go!' he said to Mr Bean with a smile on his face. 'Our little girl's OK, and we want to thank you, doctor.'

'Yes, doctor. Thank you a thousand times!' said Alison. 'What can *we* do for *you* now? We want to thank you. We'll do anything, anything . . .'

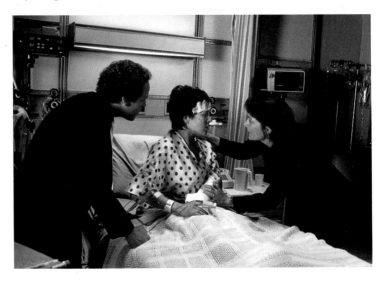

'Jennifer!' cried Alison. 'You're OK!'

Mr Bean thought for a minute. Then he took off his doctor's clothes.

'It's Mr Bean!' they shouted.

'Yes, it's me!' he said. 'And I'd like to stay with you in Los Angeles – for another week!'

Another week? With this strange Englishman? Strange – but wonderful too. Yes, Mr Bean was a friend now.

'Of course!' they all shouted. 'We love you, Mr Bean!'

Chapter 10   It's a Poster!

Mr Bean had a great week in Los Angeles. There were only one or two accidents!

The time went quickly, and then it was the end of his holiday in America. On his last day with the Langleys, they had a big party and Mr Bean took more photos of everybody. Then they had to say goodbye.

'Goodbye, *dear* Mr Bean,' said Alison and the children outside the house. 'Please come and visit us again.'

'Goodbye, everybody. Thank you very much for my lovely holiday!'

David drove Mr Bean to the airport. There were no policemen there with guns this time!

'Well, goodbye Beanie,' said David, and put his arm round him. 'Have a good journey back to England. And come back . . . some time in the future.'

David liked Mr Bean, but he remembered the bad times too!

'Goodbye, David,' said Mr Bean. 'Thank you for everything.'

Mr Bean turned and walked away. David watched him and then left the airport.

Mr Bean wanted to take one last photo . . .

Suddenly he felt somebody behind him. He turned round – and there was Mr Bean! Mr Bean wanted to take one last photo, and to put his arms round David too! Then he was ready to leave America.

◆

Three Years Later . . .

Mr Bean sat in his little house in England and thought about his wonderful holiday in America. Before he went to bed, he looked at the photos of his good friends, the Langleys, on his sitting-room wall. He smiled.

◆

In Los Angeles it was a beautiful afternoon. At the Grierson Gallery, David sat in the room with *Whistler's Mother* and thought about his strange friend, Mr Bean. He looked at the famous painting and laughed.

Suddenly, his cup of coffee began to move across the table! Then the painting began to move too!

'Oh, no!' cried David.

Mr Grierson ran into the room.

'The ground's moving, David!' he shouted. 'The paintings! What are we going to do about the paintings?'

Before David could answer, *Whistler's Mother* fell off the wall. Mr Grierson looked at the painting on the floor.

'No! No!' he suddenly cried out. 'Look, David, look!'

David looked down. On the back of the 'painting' were the words: '*Whistler's Mother* – a Grierson Gallery poster.'

'It's a *poster*, David! A *poster*! So . . . so . . . where's the painting?'

◆

. . . and to put his arms round David too!

The famous painting, Whistler's Mother, of course! With the funny face!

In England, Mr Bean got into bed. Before he went to sleep, he looked up at the wall opposite his bed and smiled.

'Goodnight, old dear!' he said, and turned off the light.

What was on the wall?

The famous painting, *Whistler's Mother*, of course! With the funny face!

ACTIVITIES

Chapters 1–3

Before you read

1 Do you know anything about Mr Bean? Look at the pictures in Chapters 1–3. Is this story going to be funny or sad?

2 Answer the questions. Find the words in *italics* in your dictionary. They are all in the story.

    a Do you like going to *art galleries*? Why/why not?

    b What *paintings* do you like? Can you *paint*?

    c Do you have any *posters* in your room? What posters?

3 Find these words in your dictionary. Write sentences with them.

    a *a handkerchief / to sneeze*

    b *sick / a sweet*

4 Find these words in your dictionary. Put them in the sentences.

    air blow fan machine seat

    a She put the dirty clothes in the washing . . . .

    b He . . . . . his nose often because he has a bad cold.

    c When it's very hot, we turn on the . . . . . in this room for some cold . . . .

    d He found his . . . . . on the plane and started reading.

After you read

5 Are these sentences right or wrong?

    a A painting by an English artist is coming to America.

    b Mr Bean is going to America because he is the most intelligent man at the National Gallery in London.

    c The police at the airport think Mr Bean has got a gun.

    d Mr Bean dances in front of the fan because the meeting is boring.

6 Work with another student. Have this conversation.

    Student A: You are David Langley. You want Mr Bean to stay in your house. Tell Alison about him.

    Student B: You are Alison Langley. You are angry with David. You want Mr Bean to stay in a hotel.

Chapters 4–7

Before you read

7 Do you think Mr Bean is going to do something to the painting? What? Discuss your ideas with another student.

8 Discuss the questions. Find the words in *italics* in your dictionary.

  a Do you like going to *fairgrounds*? Why (not)? Do you think the *rides* at fairgrounds are sometimes dangerous?

  b When you were a child, did you *ride* a bicycle? Why (not)?

  c Can you drive? Do you drive carefully when the road *surface* is wet? Why?

  d Why do people use pens and *ink* in the days of computers?

  e Where do you find *mirrors*? What do people use them for?

After you read

9 Who says these words? Who to?

  a 'You hurt a lot of people!'

  b 'I painted a face on her. Do you like it?'

  c 'I can't stop thinking about beautiful women with no clothes on!'

  d 'It's your daughter. She's in hospital.'

10 Do you like Mr Bean? Do you think he is funny or dangerous? Intelligent or stupid? Tell another student.

Chapters 8–10

Before you read

11 Do you think anybody at the Grierson Gallery will know about the poster in the future? How will they know?

12 Find these words in your dictionary. Put them in the sentences.
   bullet   operate

  a The doctor had to ..... on a woman after the road accident.

  b The ..... from the policeman's gun killed the man.

After you read

13 Which happens first? Which happens last? Write 1–4.

  a Mr Bean looks at the painting before he falls asleep.

  b Dr Jacobson thinks that Mr Bean is a doctor.

c Mr Bean takes a bullet out of a man's stomach.

d The Langleys think that Mr Bean is wonderful.

14 Who do you like in this story? Who do you not like? Why?

Writing

15 You are Mr Bean. Write about your holiday in America. What did you see and do in Los Angeles?

16 You work for the *Los Angeles Times*. Everybody now knows that the painting at the Grierson Gallery, *Whistler's Mother*, is only a poster. Who took the painting? Why? How? Where is it now? Ask David Langley questions, and then write a story for your newspaper.

17 You are Mr Bean. Write a letter to David and his family. Are they all right? And the gallery? And the poster? Tell them about your life in London.

18 Which 'accidents' did you think were funny in the story? Write about three of them.